ZERO TO SIX FIGURES

CODY ASKINS

ISBN: 978-1-64184-661-5 (Hardcover)
ISBN: 978-1-64184-662-2 (Paperback)

FOREWORD

By Lauren Askins

"If I say I am going to do something, I am going to do it."
– Cody Askins

Whoever is reading this, consider yourself fortunate. You get to learn things we have learned the hard way. Take notes and implement the steps. You will fast-track your way to success.

Cody Askins is the first guy I have ever met who can put his money where his mouth is. There have been several moments throughout the time I have known him when he has always been a person of his word. Or be able to achieve the goals he has set forth for himself.

When we first started dating, he was working for a captive insurance agency. One day Cody looked at me and said, "I am going to win the Chairman's Council trip." The next thing I knew, he made a contract, had his dad and sales manager at the time sign it, and off to the dialing he went. Cody held call nights, put miles and miles on his car, stayed the weekend in places so he could door-knock for several days in a row. You name it; he did it. And he did it with grace.

I've watched him wake up and write his goals down daily in his now tattered notebook. I am pretty sure that book has been all over the place because he doesn't tend to leave home without it. No matter the goal, Cody has this unique ability to push through difficult situations and be so disciplined in his decisions that he doesn't waiver from his goals. He challenges himself in ways that most people will not. I mean, the guy ran a ½ marathon after only training for a week. (I can promise you I've never seen him run more than maybe a mile in all our years of marriage until that day.) Then there was the half iron man that was canceled due to COVID. He sure as heck was not letting them tell him he couldn't do something that he had been looking forward to for a few months; so in true Cody fashion, he created his own race, ran in the rain and cold, all so he would be able to say he did it.

Cody Edward Askins, my Honey Bear, I love you more than you will ever truly comprehend. The day I met you, I knew you were something special. Deep in my heart, I knew you would change the world and help millions of people. I didn't know how, but I knew you were different. To say I am proud of you would be an understatement. You not only make me a better person, but you always leave anyone you meet better than you met them. You help people think bigger, work differently, and find their true potential deep inside of them. Thank you for letting me be the luckiest gal in the world to be by your side. You are my favorite.

To My Son Cody
By Brian Askins

When it comes to insurance sales training Cody is one of the very best in the industry. Cody has built multiple million dollar companies, he hosts one of the largest insurance conferences in the insurance industry, and has hosted many top retreats, which have changed lives. As Cody's dad, I could not be more proud of his accomplishments at such a young age and look forward to seeing what the future holds. What I am most proud of is his integrity, honesty, and his true love for helping others. If you are looking to go to levels you never dreamed possible, Cody is truly someone that can assist you in reaching those levels.

CONTENTS

INTRODUCTION

I *believe* we should stop playing life so small.

One day, when they say the word *insurance*, I want them to say, "That dude did more for the industry than anyone else on planet earth, *ever.*

I'm Cody Askins and I was a new agent not too long ago. I started as an intern calling out of the phonebook before I really even knew you're not supposed to be doing that. I feel like I get and understand new, struggling, sales agent. Most people in our business are not the dude making 7 figures, rollin' in it, and traveling the world. Most people in our industry are struggling... Some even have part-time jobs. All the different products, carriers, commission levels, independent or captive? Holy frick, they don't know what to do.

This is where I come in.

I want to be the guy they can really go to, to gain some knowledge and really help them. I was very fortunate to earn $117,361.13 in my first 8 months. And I thought... If I can do *that*, I can probably help other people too. I have a passion for this business, but it isn't easy, and 92% of salespeople fail within the first 3 years. But there are also more millionaires in this industry than in any industry in the world.

It's time to take back control of your life.... There is going to come a point in the next 12 months when something doesn't go your way. You'll be challenged in a way you didn't see coming. We feel like we're getting pulled underwater and we're about to drown. We can't do anything right. Nothing's going our way. We think we're going to fail. We're not sure if we can make it. We can't even afford leads, but we know we want to succeed. Eric Thomas says, "When you want to succeed as bad as you want to breathe, then you'll be successful." That's the difference between a lot of people who are successful and unsuccessful.

How badly do you want to be successful?

Will you do *whatever* it takes?

Throughout this book, I'm going to show you exactly what you need to do to make your goals and dreams a reality. It all starts with your mindset. You have to get your mind right before you can even begin and a huge part of this comes from your morning routine. I'm going to share with you my morning routine and how it helps me to jump-start my day, every day. You have to be in the right frame of mind if you're going to survive in this business.

But I don't want you to just survive, I want you to thrive.

Part of thriving is setting goals. Goals are one of the most important things you can ever have and do for yourself. Without goals, you're just driving around aimlessly with no destination. So I'm going to show you how to set goals and push yourself further than you've ever dreamed possible. I'll also give you tools along the way to achieve those goals.

I'm going to show you how to be confident and how to be consistent when it comes to getting in front of prospects and making sales. We are going to go in-depth on how to handle objections so you can literally tackle anything they throw at you. And I mean anything, just ask my team. You *might* even pick up some tips on how to handle the dreaded, "Where do you want to go to dinner?" question. And by the time we're done, you'll be a master at closing because we are going to cover multiple types of closes so you will have a full arsenal in your toolbelt. I'm telling you, there won't be anything that you can't handle.

I know this all sounds fantastic, incredible, and amazing. I'm telling you now, this isn't going to be a walk in the park, it won't be easy. You have to have commitment and dedication.

But I'm here to help you by taking out all the guesswork. I'll show you how to be successful at working the phone, how to build those underrated but oh-so-important relationships with your prospects. And most importantly, how to make it all make sense for you to make the money you've always wanted.

You're in the right place and I can tell you're serious. I believe the most important thing to be successful in this business is when agents, like yourself right now, spend money and take time to invest in themselves. We are building a massive following in the insurance industry to *help* agents. And I want to help you.

CHAPTER 1

Get Your Mindset Right

Whatever you want to have, you have to decide to go get it. Read that again. Whatever *YOU* want to have, *YOU* have to decide to go get it.

I fully believe this, always have, and always will. No one is going to do it for you and no one is going to give it to you. Nobody said, "Here Cody let me give you leads. Let me give you motivation and dedication. Let me fuel your desire and passion for more." No one did that for me and no one is going to do it for you either. Sure you might have some amazing people in your corner cheering you on, and if you do, that's amazing! This is something that will be incredibly helpful. But even the biggest cheerleader won't *make* you do something. They won't make you show up when things suck and it feels like nothing is going your way. They won't. Showing up is something that has to come from you. It has to come from your desire to do more and to be more.

Consistency is the name of this game, of any game really. Are you going to show up and be consistent? If you're not, best of luck to you. But if you're willing to do the work, I'm willing to help you.

So right now you need to make the decision to show up in order to go up.

I know you can do it, I see it every day in my office. I see these guys coming in when they're sick or when yesterday was the worst day they've had in a long, long time. When all the normal things they try just don't seem to be working, but there is one thing that always will, consistency and showing up for yourself.

First things first, I highly recommend a morning routine. I know some people don't believe in them and I know others (myself included) live and die by them. Having a morning routine, adding structure to my day, and utilizing very specific things to kick-start my day have been instrumental in my success. I'm going to show you the morning routine I adhere to every day. I call this my "Daily Power 5," and I commit to it seven days a week. (Yes, I said seven!)

Daily Power 5

The 5 AM Club.

The first step in my "Daily Power 5" is waking up between 5:00 - 5:59 a.m. every morning. We call this *The 5 AM Club.* For some of you, this will be easy. For others, it won't. It's the little adjustments we make and pushing ourselves that will propel us from good to great. I believe if it's meant to be it's up to me. Sales is a mental game and only a struggle if you make it one. Mental toughness is everything. Welcome to the club.

Work Out.

Get your blood pumping and your body moving!

Having a hard workout first thing in the morning is exactly what I need to wake myself up and get prepared for the day ahead. A daily morning workout helps get your energy level up, get you focused and in the right frame of mind. In this business, I believe that mindset *is EVERYTHING.* If you don't push yourself no one else will.

Write Down Your Goals.
Everyone should have goals. If you don't know where you are going you won't get there. Are you staying stagnant or are you pushing for more? With a 92% failure rate in insurance sales, being average just isn't cutting it. If you didn't have goals to achieve great things, you wouldn't be reading this book. Starting today, and every single day after this, you need to write down what you want to accomplish. Don't just think about it; write it down. It's amazing what starts to happen when you set it, write it down every day, and focus on making it a reality.

When goal-setting, you want to look at the short term, long term, and anything else you want to accomplish. For example, set goals for every month, year, and long term - something you will accomplish someday. These could be what your income is going to be every month and year. Or what you want it to increase to every month. Just make sure you are writing them down and pushing yourself to think bigger. Here are some of my personal goals:

1. 8% Nation has 10,000 agents in attendance.

2. We sell $1,000,000 every 30 days.

3. We generate over 100M in total company revenue.

4. We own a beach house, a vision jet, and a helicopter.

5. We own 1,000 apartment units.

Writing down my goals every day keeps me humble and always thinking bigger.

Learning and Training.
One of the keys to growth is learning and the day we stop learning is the day we stop growing. I make it a point to learn something new every single day. Not only to learn something

new but, to physically train or role-play so that you can apply it in the near future. I do this by watching videos, reading books, listening to podcasts and audiobooks. Just stay open to new information and always be willing to learn.

The other key aspect of learning is training. Once I've learned something new I can incorporate it into my training videos or put it on my YouTube channel. Another of my favorite things to do is to role-play what I've learned. This is something that we do in my office twice a day. The quickest way to master something new is to train and practice it every single day.

Cold Shower.
I end every shower with a cold shower. Did you just cringe? I know you did. Most people will read through the first four items of my "Daily Power 5" thinking that this is easy enough to do. But a cold shower? Why Cody?

The very obvious answer is, that this is a great way to wake up. But here's the thing, and hear me out. This forces me to do something I don't want to do. Now you're probably thinking, why would I force myself to do something I don't want to do in the first place? When you are forced to do something you don't want to do, the next time something else comes up that you don't want to do, you'll be more likely to do it. A perfect example is making just one more sales call. If you've had a bad day and you can't imagine making one more call, you'll have to force yourself to pick up the phone. Forcing yourself to make one more call, could mean the difference between making a sale or not. So end every shower with a cold shower, step outside your comfort zone and do something you don't want to do to start your day.

As I said earlier, I highly recommend a daily routine. It's powerful, beneficial, and needed. It's so important to get yourself in the right frame of mind. By keeping your energy up, staying focused, and working on your mindset the days that don't go your way won't be that big of a deal. You'll be more positive and it will be easier to just let things roll right off your back. By staying positive you'll be able to power through.

But how does one stay more positive Cody? Great question... I have some tips and tricks for that too.

One way to do that is to focus on the things you *can* control. Every salesperson has certain things that are out of their control, but there are always things they can control. Such as, how many cold calls did you make today? How many appointments did you set up for next week? Did you decide to skip door-knocking because you aren't comfortable with it yet, or did you force yourself to do something uncomfortable (like that cold shower)?

This is not all-inclusive to sales, this is a life hack right here. There are always things you will be in control of, like what time you wake up in the morning, getting that workout in no matter how much you want to skip it, and writing down those goals.

You will have days when you don't want to do any of it. I still do. But I also still *make* myself go through all of my morning routine. All of these things are part of adopting the right mindset. But it goes even further than that. Let's focus on what you can control. I like to call these my "Three A's Within Your Control." The first being 'Attitude'.

3 A's Within Your Control

Attitude.
Right now I want you to take a second and think about your attitude. Is your attitude positive? Or do you have a tendency to be a negative person who is always complaining? I also want you to think about the things that support you in having a *positive attitude*. If working out causes you to have a better attitude, then don't you think you should probably

work out (not to mention it is part of the Daily Power 5)? What else puts you in the right frame of mind?

Having the right frame of mind, or a positive attitude determines how well you will do. Now does that mean you are going to have a good day every day? No. But by having a good attitude when something doesn't go the way you planned, it will make it easier to bounce back. Something I do every day is checking my attitude on my way into the office. Am I in the right frame of mind? Am I being a good example? If not, I shift my mindset because this is something I can control.

Action.
The second 'A' stands for Action, you can even think of it as *activity*. What is the *action* or *activity* you are putting forth? If I ask you to dial 100 numbers this is something that you *can* do. This is something that you *can control*. You may not want to dial 100 numbers but you can. It is within your control. If you control the action then you can control your outcome.

Attention.
The last of the three A's that you can control is how *attentive* or the amount of *focus* you have. What I mean by this is always being in the moment. Are you fully in the moment? Are you present? Are you in the right frame of mind? Are you being intentional? When I was playing basketball, one thing my father always used to tell me was, he could always tell that my focus was on point when I got down and slapped the floor on defense. I was in the zone. What do you do to make sure you are in the zone and ready? Are you giving it your full attention and firing on all cylinders?

All these things are completely within your control. Since they are within your control you should work to control them every day. When you show up with the right frame of mind

ZERO TO SIX FIGURES

and control the things you can, it is amazing how well you can do.

When it comes to sales anybody can be good at it. But why be good in sales when you can be the best? Why have a crappy attitude when you can have a positive one? Because when your attitude is positive, when you're doing the things you can control, I promise you, you'll see more outcomes going your way. But let's take it a step further.

Every great salesperson has a very specific set of qualities. I've seen many veteran salespeople who, when missing just one of these qualities, don't produce nearly the results they're capable of achieving. To go from good to great, there are a few things every salesperson needs to have. I call these the "8 C's Every Great Salesperson Has."

8 C's Every Great Salesperson Has

Coachable

Are you coachable? Do you want to get better? I would take a bad salesperson who is coachable over a great salesperson with an ego. I've seen a lot of great salespeople that don't make it in this company because they let their ego get in the way - they just aren't coachable and that is their downfall. Great people know that they can always improve so in order to succeed you have to be coachable. How coachable are you?

Courage

Do you have the courage to do what it takes to succeed in this business? How willing are you to do what it takes to hit your goals? Are you willing to do the hard stuff? Or are you going to turn tail and run as soon as it gets hard? You have to have the courage to step outside of your comfort zone. Remember, cold shower.

Don't like making phone calls? Do it anyway. Don't like knocking doors in a retirement community? Do it anyway.

When you have the courage to step up and do what others aren't willing to do, things that make you uncomfortable, that is when you make the magic happen. That is when you hit those goals. That is when you become unstoppable. So step up and stand out.

Commitment

To be successful in sales you have to be committed. How committed are you? Show up. Do the work. If you love the product and believe in the product you're going to make a difference in your client's lives. You have to believe in what you're selling. I believe that wholeheartedly. You have to believe it too. If you don't, then this isn't for you. And this is why 92% fail within the first three years. Because they aren't committed.

Be committed to going that extra mile. Are you showing up every day? Are you doing what it takes to grow? Are you committed to learning and improving yourself? Are you challenging yourself to be better? Every. Single. Day. I want you to ask yourself right now, how committed are you? Did you give it your all and leave everything on the table, or could you have done more? Could you have pushed harder? Be committed and I promise you, you'll see results.

Control

As a salesperson, you have to be in control, if you aren't that means that the prospect is in control. This *does not* mean you have the gift of gab and you talk the entire time. I make more sales when the prospect talks more than I do. I can be in control of the call and not be the one talking. You ask the questions. You gain control. You steer the path of the conversation. This is how you take control and you must be in control. It's a feeling. You can tell if you aren't in control and if you are not in control you will not make the sale.

When that happens you just have to bring it back. It's just like in basketball when the forward's dominant dribble is to the right side. To take control you just turn them to the left. One shift is all it takes.

Confident

Next is confidence - great salespeople are naturally confident. You've been around them before and you know what I'm talking about, the personal swag they have, and the way they carry themselves. You can be confident while still being humble. They take charge, it is as if they are saying, "I am confident in my ability to get it done. I am confident in the company. I am confident in the product or service. I am confident that I have the ability to make this sale." Confidence is key.

Certainty

Certainty is another level of confidence. I am certain that I will make this sale. I am certain this is a service that they need. I am certain they will answer the call. When you get certain about the fact that you should make this sale right now OR you are doing the prospect and their family a massive disservice, that is a whole other level of believability. When you get to this point of certainty you will make sales that you don't think you will make.

A perfect example of this is, one of our salespeople had followed up with a prospect 20 times. They sent 5 emails and had 15 phone calls and couldn't get her to buy. I said, "Look at me. Say right now out loud, I will get it done on this call. She is going to buy and I'm *certain* it is going to happen." He said it, got on the phone, and made the sale. All because he believed on *another* level. When you believe on a *certainty* level it's amazing. You can end up getting people to buy that you never thought you could sell.

Consistent

These are the salespeople that show up every day whether they want to or not. They make the calls whether they want to or not. These are the people that put in the work no matter what. They show up and they are consistent day in and day out for long periods of time. They say great salespeople make decisions quickly but change things slowly. They don't change their consistency or their output on a day-to-day basis. They show up for long periods of time. It's like my coaches used to say, "long obedience in the same direction." When this happens you have a better chance of getting the sale and a better chance of getting great long term.

Conviction

When you know what you are talking about. When you believe what you are saying and you *KNOW* it to be true with every fiber of your being, this is conviction. You can feel it. The prospect can feel it. Now you are taking your conviction and making them believe it. This is taking believability to the next level. When the prospect believes, because you believe so strongly that you believe enough for both of you, that's conviction.

These are the 8 C's that every great salesperson has and that YOU need to have to be great at sales too. If you read through all of these and are thinking dang, I don't have all of these Cody! Don't worry. You can develop them. Anyone *can* be coachable, it's all about your approach to things. Try thinking about life the way you did when you were a kid. You always had questions and you were always wanting to learn more. Adopt that "beginner" mindset and you will become coachable.

Do the stuff that scares you, especially if it scares you. When you make a commitment, honor it. If you aren't good at doing that, don't make hard-to-keep commitments. Start with the small stuff. That's something you can control.

Speaking of control, honestly, this should be a breeze by now. Confidence on the other hand isn't just something people are innately born with, sure it happens, but you can train yourself to be confident. Learn material, PRACTICE what you've learned. When you've practiced and rehearsed 100 times the only option is for you to get better. This is the same thing for certainty, you'll get to a level of confidence where you're just certain you're going to be a rockstar.

Speaking of awesomeness... I've got some more ways for you to up your sales game in the next section. If you're ready to really dig in, let's take it to the next level together.

Taking It To The Next Level

Motivation

These are some tips I try to do every single day and they pay off. Everyone gets bored and complacent from time to time. I'm no different. But there are several things that you can do to overcome this when you notice you're in a rut.

When you eat healthy food, you feel good. When I feel good, I sell better. Do I love having a footlong chili cheese dog from Sonic? Who doesn't from time to time? But how am I going to go to someone's house after eating all of that and sell? You can't sell if you're in a food coma because you need to be focused. If I'm not focused I'm not the best Cody Askins I can be because I'm not at my peak. To make you, the best you that you possibly can be, you need to eat healthy food. I always feel better after eating a healthy meal instead of feeling bogged down and heavy.

The second tip is to work out—do something. I'm not saying you have to spend hours killing it in the gym. Typically I work out 30-60 minutes a day but starting out it wasn't that way. I love the energy I get from it. If your stamina isn't up to working out at that level or for that long yet, all you need is 5 minutes first thing in the morning. If I do 5 different exercises for 1 minute each I can tell a huge difference in my energy and mindset. And I can't make an excuse for not working out or doing something for 5 minutes. If I can't do something for 5 minutes then I'm lazy. So don't be lazy, there is no reason you can't do something for 5 minutes a day. Make sure you are putting your focus on improving yourself and showing up for yourself. If you do, it will show up in your sales, in your work ethic, and your attitude.

The third tip is reading or listening to something that makes you better, makes you learn something, and challenges you. Soak up something so you're improving yourself and you're learning. It is so, so important to read or listen to something. That is something great people do. And we might as well pattern ourselves after people who've been great. After people who are the top salespeople in the world, the top individuals in the world. I want to pattern myself after someone who's awesome and great so that I too can be awesome and great.

The fourth tip is writing your goals down. You don't have to be perfect at it, I'm not but it's a great success tip. I write my goals down every day. Write down big goals too, I'm not talking about these little dinky goals. I'm talking big freaking massive goals. I'm talking about goals that when you wake up you jump out of bed because you're so excited to get to the office, to get in front of prospects, and sell. I'm talking about goals like mine where my company will be a 100 million dollar company one day. A lot of people will doubt me but I've got goals and I'm going to stick to them!

What are your goals?
Write them down every morning. Throw in a long-term goal, a short-term goal, and any other goals you want. I always have a goal for every month, every year, and long-term. Like every month I have a goal that I want my income to increase and I write it down. I also write down what I want

my income to be for the year. By writing down your goals you start to think bigger, I'm telling you it's infectious! Our brains think so small. We are capable of sooo much more. When we start thinking *big*, it's un-freaking real how capable we are of doing massive stuff. I promise you in 10 years I will look back on the Cody Askins today and say that Cody thought small. I promise you because I'll be thinking so big by then, that this Cody is a chump compared to the Cody of the future.

So the success tips are to eat healthy food, work out, read or listen to something, and write down your goals. If you do this I promise you, it will affect you in a positive way. It will change you. It will make you the best YOU, that you can be. If you're serious about success you will implement these right away. So that you can be, the best you that you possibly can be. I want you to be great! I want you to be awesome! I want what you're reading here to take you to the next level! If you implement these things along with all the other content you've been learning then 100k, 250k, half a million dollars, a million dollars it doesn't matter. You can achieve any of it. I promise you.

How to Work With Prospects

People are the key to this business. You can't sell insurance to a dog. You have to sell to people. And to sell to them, you have to know how to work with them. What makes them tick? What are their habits? What are the things they are absolutely going to do when you're trying to sell them? Let's find out...

5 Ways to Prospect Without Being Pushy
To hit these great goals, most salespersons think that you have to be extremely pushy or aggressive, but you don't. There is a way to be aggressive in sales but to do it in a respectful

way that doesn't feel like you are being aggressive or pushy. I have 5 different ways to prospect and sell more and capitalize on sales without being pushy. Prospects can feel when you are being pushy. Just like if you are smiling on the phone with them, they can feel your smile. They can feel if you have their best interest in mind. They can feel if you are trying to sell them. So what do you do instead?

Remove The Pressure
You are there to educate and inform them. It is your job to provide them with information. Let them know that if they do business or not with you, that's okay. They don't have to do anything today. Ask them what it was that got them thinking about life insurance (or whatever it is you are trying to sell them). Now you have moved around the objection and have proceeded on the path to selling. Just remember to remove the pressure so it doesn't feel like a high-pressure situation. *YOU* are their *PROBLEM SOLVER*. It needs to feel like you are educating, informing, and assisting them. Do some things that will take the pressure off and put them at ease. This could be as simple as where to sit in the room or accepting a glass of water they offer you. Anything that you can do so during the sale that doesn't feel like you are hardcore selling yourself.

Take Your Time
All sales for me are typically 45 minutes to an hour and a half. I'm in no hurry because building a relationship is the most important piece of a sale. So slow down, be relaxed, make sure you are getting to know them, and warm-up. Take this time to fact find *BEFORE* you present and close. You don't want to give them a quote in the first 2 minutes or the first 4 minutes of being there. I'm not trying to sell them. This is selling without being pushy. Once you realize that

relationship is the most important thing to any sale, you're on your way.

Let The Prospect Do The Talking

This is by far my favorite one. People think that to be good at sales and selling that I need to talk a lot, or puke, vomit and regurgitate a ton of words or say this special phrase. You don't. You do not need to have the gift of gab. You simply need to let them talk. Remember that the person doing most of the talking is not always in control of the conversation. This is a myth, you need *them* talking.

Typically when my prospect talks more than I do, I make the sale. When I talk more than they do, I don't sell because I'm trying to tell them instead of simply asking questions. I believe I should let them talk. If you focus on and think like that, you actually ask questions and listen. Then they will tell you why you are going to be selling them. If you let them communicate in that way, they will tell you everything you need to know.

The key to this is to ASK GREAT QUESTIONS. Ask open-ended questions like, *"What got you thinking about this? When do you plan on doing something like this? What does this look like for you? If you were to do it in one year from now what would your business (or personal life) look like?"* You want to get them thinking and talking. The whole point of a sale is that it is a path to take them from point A to point B. As an agent, I'm asking questions to get you to where you are literally selling yourself.

Make Your Prospect Feel Comfortable

Some of you may be wondering how to do this? We've talked about it. Build the relationship, use humor, ask the right questions, talk about their family, TALK ABOUT THINGS THEY WANT TO TALK ABOUT.

Agents like to think people buy because of how great we are, or how great our company is, or the product. **PROSPECTS DON'T CARE.** They don't buy price, products, or the company. They buy... what do they buy? Think about it for a second....

YOU. They buy you because you provide a solution. They buy your commitment. They buy the belief that you will help them in a certain way. They are buying into you. Your belief, conviction, and confidence. They will end up buying you. But remember, this won't happen instantly. Not in the first 2 minutes, not in the first 4 minutes, it will take *time* because they will need to feel comfortable. You need to smile, to laugh, and you need to chill the freak out sometimes instead of being so over the top salesy and aggressive. So stop acting crazy, just pause... Take a step back and say, if this was going to take 1 hour what would the next hour look like? Not you beating them up for an hour. That's not how sales work.

Focus On Their Problems, Not Your Product

Focus on what your product can do FOR them, not the actual product. Think about what you being there selling them this solution, can do *for them*. Because that is all you are doing when you are in sales, you are selling them a *solution* to their *problem*. This means you better believe in your product and what it can do for them. You better have that confidence and that certainty in your product.

Do not confuse this with talking *about* your product. When you are talking about your product you're being selfish and greedy and talking about yourself. Talk about the *SOLUTION and THEM*. How this can help them. How this can solve their problems. If they are worried about final expenses being covered, what their income will be if their husband passes away, paying off their mortgage, then these are the things you should be talking about! If they are worried about getting cancer, some other health issue, or their car blowing up. These are the problems you've told me about in your life and we have these solutions to solve your problems.

No one wants a pushy, aggressive salesperson that isn't listening to them. Someone who is just trying to push a product on them. Don't be that salesperson.

We've covered a lot of ground here in chapter 1. So let's do a quick recap and write this awesomeness down, it will help. Start with your morning, do you have a morning routine or not? If not, make one. If you already have one, great - how well does it align to the *Daily Power 5?* If it doesn't, tweak it until it does. Are you in the 5 AM club? Are you working out? Do you write down your goals? Are you learning new things every day and training on the things you've learned? Are you pushing yourself to do something that you don't want to do, like that cold shower? I see you shaking your head, now make your adjustments and move forward.

Making those adjustments to your daily morning routine should help to get you into the right frame of mind but in case it doesn't, make sure you check your attitude. While you are checking things, what is your action or activity level like? Are you slacking or leaving it all on the table as we talked about? When you are doing the things that you need to be doing are you focused and present - are you attentive? If not, you know what you need to do.

How coachable are you? Are you going to read this and think, "Yeah, I got this Cody." Or are you going to take what I'm telling you and put it to use to work for you? Do you have the courage and the commitment to do what it takes every day, day in and day out? Are you calling 100 people a day and controlling the things you can? Or are you slacking? Are you confident, certain, and consistent? Do you have the conviction that it takes to close your sales?

Last, when it comes to prospecting how are you measuring up? Remember to remove the pressure, take your time to build that relationship with them, and let them do the talking but stay in control of the conversation. Put them at ease and make them feel comfortable, you're a human, not a robot so don't act like one. Don't forget to focus on their problems and how you can be a problem solver for them.

CHAPTER 2

Goals That Work

Let's talk more about goal setting because this is so important we can't talk about it enough. Every successful person does this. To be successful you have to set goals and I don't mean just any goals, let's get specific. This is how I made $117,361.13 in my first year of sales at 19 years old.

During orientation when I was starting as a new agent, a veteran agent asked all 10 of us to stand up. Then he pointed to someone else and told them to stay standing and asked everyone else to sit down. I was one of the agents who were told to sit down. He told us that maybe one of us would make it. In those moments I made a commitment to myself that I was going to make it and I would make $100k my first year. I then wrote it on a piece of paper, dated it, and signed the paper. I put that piece of paper in my cubicle and I looked at this paper every day. Eight months later, I hit my goal of earning $100k from cold calling and door knocking with no purchased leads. Cold calling and door knocking are THE hardest ways to get sales. But I set that goal and I was determined to hit it.

Let's talk about the specifics of goal setting. The first thing you do when goal setting is to set your target. What is it that you want to accomplish? When I set this goal of making 100k in the first year I didn't say, 'I'd like to make 100k.' Or 'I want to make 100k.'

I said *I WILL earn 100k this year.*

I AM going to earn 100k this year.

These are specific goals, notice I didn't say 'I might', 'probably', 'I may'.... No. I AM going to... then date it and sign it. This is your commitment to yourself. The easiest person to lie to... is you. Set specific goals, and hold yourself accountable.

Now that you have your goal for the year, break it down into a monthly, weekly, and daily goal. If you want to make $100k divide that by 50 weeks (taking two weeks for vacation). You will need to earn $2,000 a week. It is much easier to focus on making $2,000 a week than $100k a year.

Know your numbers.

Once you know you need to earn $2,000 per week to hit your $100k goal, how much will you need to sell each day? My average per sale amount was $400 - $500 per sale. That meant I needed to make 5 sales a week in commission to reach my $2,000 target. This is why I stress knowing your numbers so you can utilize my Set/Sit/Sale model.

For me to earn $2,000, knowing my average sale is $400 - $500, I needed to *Set* 15 appointments each week. Of those 15 appointments, I had to *Sit* with 10 and *Sell* 5 out of the 10. Now, your numbers may be different than mine. But I knew if I was sitting with 10 appointments that I was selling 5 of those appointments. So figure out what your numbers are so you can break them down and accomplish your goals on a daily basis.

When should I set my goals? Every Sunday night I prepare and write down my plan of action for the week. *I will earn $2,000 this week.* Take it seriously. I know some of you won't, but if you *do* it will pay off. If you are preparing for the week and setting yourself up, you can string together a phenomenal year one week at a time. When you have one good week here and another good week after that, you build momentum. Make sure you win each week. When you string enough wins together on a week-by-week basis this is how you will win the year.

This applies to me, too. When you look at me, you hear my story, you see how far I've come and you might think I've made it. But I haven't. Here are some of the goals I'm working towards right now.

1. 8% Nation has 10,000 agents in attendance.

2. We sell $1,000,000 every 30 days.

3. We generate over 100M in total company revenue.

4. We own a beach house, a vision jet, and a helicopter.

5. We own 1,000 apartment units.

Am I there yet? Nope. ***I haven't arrived yet and I hope I never do.***

Wait, what? I haven't arrived yet and I hope I never do. Because when I've arrived it means I've stopped setting goals and growing and I NEVER want that to happen.

I don't want you to fall short either. Set a goal. Then set it bigger. Now it's time to reverse engineer your goal. If you're striving for $500,000 a year, break it down by the month, week, and day. Know your numbers. Know what it takes.

Activity
What does it take to make it happen? If you want that $500,000 a year and you make twenty appointments a week, is that enough? If fifteen of them follow through, and you complete eight sales a week, is that enough? Does that get you to your goal? How many people do you need to call to

get those twenty appointments? What specific activity will it take to get you to your weekly goal?

It's not enough to work through this goal process. You have to write it down. Write down your goals daily. Just like I did mine above. Write them down *DAILY*.

You might look at my goals and think they're too big. But will I own a jet someday? Abso-freakin-lutely. Will I reach $1,000,000 a month? Of course, probably before I own a jet. Will there be 10,000 attendees at our conference? Probably within a few years. Will I help every salesperson in the world? Only time will tell.

The point is that when I started out, I set much smaller goals. Now every time I work through the goal-setting process, I think bigger. I see what it took to reach my smaller goals, and I continue to strive for more. I am committed to going bigger and helping more people.

I want to challenge you in your own business to set goals just like mine because I'm not special. If I can do this, so can you. And I *am* doing it! Can you reach goals like this? Absolutely.

But to do it, you'll have to be creative. You'll have to think on another level and be innovative. When I first started in the industry, I got groups of college students together on Monday nights to do cold calling. I paid them $10 for the first two appointments they set and $20 for each appointment after that. I trained them and coached them through calls. I even got them pizza and gave out gift cards through the night. Then I gave $100 to the person who set me the most appointments for the week. I'm not saying you have to do this, but be creative.

When I ran out of activity to do, I would go door-knocking on a Friday night at a senior living facility, and knock on 50, 60, 80 sometimes even 125 doors. If you're like dude, no way am I doing that. This doesn't have to be one of your methods but you need some kind of activity so you can hit your weekly numbers. When you know your numbers and are doing whatever it takes to hit those numbers you have a better chance of hitting your long-term goals.

You also have to be committed to learning from other people. Go to conferences and retreats, watch videos, seek out a mentor, and never stop growing your business. Do whatever it takes. Even if that means you have to cold call or door knock. Pick up the phone. This is one of the hardest things for agents to do. Just pick up the phone and you've already done more than most are willing to do.

Think about your last year and what you can learn from it. Then look into the future at your next year. Set your goals and then think about every potential problem that could come up and take them all away. What would hold you back from hitting your goal? It's important to know because it's probably going to happen, and you need to be prepared.

Once you've set your goals, reverse engineer them, break down your goals, and make a plan of attack. Eliminate the excuses and put in the work. Think about a year from now. What will it take to reach that goal? Get it done. I promise you that a year from now, the feeling of success will be worth whatever work you had to put in.

What's it going to take every day and every week to get there?

Create a weekly outline that breaks down what it takes to reach your big goal for the year. Write down your goals every morning and every night to get your mind focused and to get you hyped up. Strive for more and don't settle.

If you find that week after week, you're falling behind where you want to be, reassess your goals. This doesn't mean lowering them. Never, ever lower your goals. When I tell you to reassess, I mean that you should reassess your processes and flow. What is working for you and what isn't? Are you

dialing enough numbers? Are you setting enough appointments? How can you improve closing your sales? Find ways
to duplicate your success and tweak the things that aren't
working until you see improvements.

CHAPTER 3

Handling Objections

If you can handle objections (and I know you can), you will become unstoppable. Here's how to do it in five minutes. A lot of objections are human nature. Think about it. You walk into Best Buy and when the salesperson asks you what you're looking for or if they can help you find anything, what do you say? "No, I'm just looking." Or "I'm just shopping." It is human nature to say no or give an objection, even when you don't really mean it.

Here is another example. Whenever I ask my wife, "Hey babe, where do you want to go to dinner?" What do you think she says?

"Ah, no." Or, "I don't know." "I'm not sure."

"Well okay babe, if you had to choose one place to go for dinner tonight, where would you go?"

This is something I use all the time. I agree or acknowledge the objection and then redirect the conversation by asking the right question. These are two of the 3 A's you should use when handling objections. Let's talk about all 3 in more detail.

3 A's to Handling Objections

Agree
Psychology tells us that people will give an objection early in a call or interaction. It is how we are wired. When someone gives you an objection they do not mean the objection they are giving you. In sales when we hear an objection, most of us are trained to hammer them with the information. But that's disagreeable. It's combative. It challenges them. And the number one rule of sales is to *agree*.

Think about it. What's the best way to de-escalate a situation or conflict in anything?

Agree.

My wife and I will be fighting and I'll say, "You know what babe, you're right."

She'll say, "You know I wish you would stop agreeing with me."

"I thought that's what you wanted. Right?"

Be agreeable. It de-escalates and allows you to move on.

Answer
After you've agreed with the objection, you want to answer the objection. Here is a common conversation you'll hear:

> Prospect: "Hey I don't know that I can qualify. I'm in bad health."
> Agent: "I understand. And hey, thank you so much for sharing that. This program is actually meant for people that are not in great health."

You have *agreed* with their objection by saying that you understand and you thanked them for sharing that information. Then you are *answering* their objection by stating the program is meant for them. Once you answer their objection, the objection they *thought* they had, goes away. It just disappears. But you cannot forget to follow it up with the right questions.

Ask

The psychology is if I don't finish with a question, *and* I just *agree* and *answer* then they are going to restate their original objection. Or they are going to hang up. But if I finish with a question, I am reassuming control of the call. I'm trying to get back on script, and I'm trying to proceed down the finish line. You should never respond to a fake objection or a "real objection", if you believe those exist, without finishing with a question. *Agree. Answer. Ask.*

Real-Life Situations

Let's go through some real-life situations so you can see how to handle objections.

Joplin Missouri

I used this at an appointment in Joplin, Missouri years ago. I said, "Sir, do you know where your life insurance policy is?"

Like everyone it's human nature to say 'no' and 'I don't know.' So he said, "I don't know." Some of you would have **believed** that he didn't know if or where his policy was. I said something that made zero sense, and I still use it to this day.

I said, "Sir *if* you knew where your life insurance policy was, where would it be?"

He said, "Well if I knew where it was, it would be in the filing cabinet right over there." pointing across the room.

I said, "This one," as I walked over and pointed to the filing cabinet. He nodded.

"Okay. I said, "Top or bottom drawer?"

He said, "Probably the top."

"Can I open it?"

"Yes."

I opened the top drawer of the filing cabinet, guess what was sitting right there on the top drawer? His insurance policy. But 8 seconds before when I asked him where it was he said, "I don't know." It's human nature to have an objection. In the psychology of sales, the number one thing when dealing with objections is to always agree.

Life Insurance Policy
When consulting for an insurance company in New York, they told me their prospects were saying they didn't want to talk to agents about Life Insurance because it gives them the "heebeegeebees."
My response? Excellent!
Tell the client, "I agree! I'm with you. Talking about Life Insurance gives me the heebeegeebees too. I hate talking about it. However, with everything going on in the world, you'd be amazed at how many people are trying to qualify for life insurance right now. And I want to make sure we didn't leave you out. So tell me, who do you currently have your life insurance with, outside of work?"
Boom. That's agreeing. It's not natural because most salespersons are not trained that way.
When someone says, "I'm not interested." we respond aggressively.
New agents will say, "Well what do you mean you're not interested? You don't have enough information to be interested yet."
This is our first response because that's how we've been trained. When what we should do is *agree* with them.
When they say they aren't interested, *THEY* showed interest in speaking with you and responded to your call. When they say they don't have any money, homeless people have money. Right? Because I give it to them, sometimes. Right?

When they say that they already have coverage - that's fantastic! That's awesome. They believe in the product so 'they're more likely to talk to me about it. Now, let's put all of this into practice with common objections you'll hear in the field.

Role-Playing

Every single morning I have my team train, we role-play. I ask each one of them, what is the most frequent objection you get. I want one that is so freaking false, to begin with? What is the biggest objection you've received? How do you rebuttal the false objections people give you?

If you give validity and acknowledge the objection, you are making the objection more 'real' to them. They didn't mean it, right? It's freaking fake. So we role play back and forth and we put our agents on the spot. We want to make sure they are prepared for when they will come face to face with a false objection.

If I were role-playing with you right now, I would say, "Hey I'm busy. I'm going into a meeting, call me back. Can you call me back?"

Agent: "Perfect. I'll be very brief. Let me ask you a quick question."

Boom. Then, instead of pausing, ask a question. Pausing shows a lack of confidence like you don't know what to say. You don't know what to do. Or you aren't ready for the call. If you ever hesitate or struggle with what to say, then you've gotta freakin' role play. Every. Single. Day.

Objections

I'm Busy

People don't answer the phone when they're busy. If they were truly freaking' busy, they don't have time to answer their phone. Here is how the call should go:

> Prospect: "I'm busy."
> Agent: "I totally understand. I get it. Everyone is so busy these days. Let me ask you a quick question."

I'm Not Interested

> Prospect: "I'm not interested."
> Agent: "I understand. It's my job to simply get you the information since you requested it. Now I'm going to be out in your area on Friday. Should I just drop it off in the morning or the afternoon? Which is better for you?"

I'm Already Insured

> Prospect: "I'm already insured. My daughter takes care of that."
> Agent: "Excellent. I promise you'll get to talk to your daughter. So tell me again, how do you spell your last name again?"—Ask the question to get back on track and take control of the conversation.

Put It In The Mail

> Prospect: "Just put it in the mail."
> Agent: "Absolutely. Hey, it looks like I'll be out your way in the next couple of days. I'll bring it with me. Does morning or afternoon work better for you?"

I Won't Qualify

> Prospect: "I won't qualify." Or, "I don't think I qualify."

Agent: "I totally understand. A lot of people have that concern. What is it that makes you think you wouldn't qualify?

I Can't Afford It

Prospect: "I can't afford it."

Agent: "I totally understand that. We have a lot of different payment options. Does $50 a month sound okay or would $40 work better for you?"

I'm Going Into A Meeting

Prospect: "You'll have to call me back. I'm heading into a meeting."

Agent: "Totally understand. I'll be very brief. Let me ask you a quick question." Then ask a question.

Voicemail/Text/Email

The following can be applied to leaving a voicemail, sending a text, or an email. You can always use a normal script and leave a voicemail. Just remember to always make it concise and make it simple.

Saying something like, "Hey Betty, it's Cody I'm just getting back to you. You requested the information I'm just calling here to give it to you now. I'll be out in your area, call me back as soon as you can."

Or I would say, "Hey Betty, getting back to you for your request for the new information. Hey, I've got some *GREAT NEWS*! I want to give that to you, call me back as soon as you possibly can." Leave the phone number twice. That's a 'good news' call which is phenomenal and gets a lot of calls back.

It could also be the 'quick question' call. "Hey, Miss Betty. I got your call, I just have one really *quick question* call me back as soon as you possibly can." Leave the phone number twice.

If you've called them a bunch of times and you can't get ahold of them, try this fourth variation:

"Hey, I noticed we haven't heard back from you, no big deal. We went ahead and processed your information. If you have any questions about what we processed, you can call us. Here is our number...." give the number twice. That's "processing" it and that's good for when you're working the phone. They will panic that you're processing their information and they *will* return the call.

Or try this face-to-face option. "Hey Miss Betty, we haven't heard from you. We are just going to deliver it and drop it off to you. I'll be out in your area in the next couple of days and I'll see you then. If you don't want me to do that, call me."

You can see there are a ton of ways to do this. Just remember to keep it simple, agree, answer, and ask. Agree with whatever their objection is so they know you're on their side. Answer whatever objection they think they have to remove the objection. Then follow up by taking control of the conversation by asking an open-ended question. If you do this, *agree/answer/ask,* you'll be able to handle any objection that comes your way. Remember to role play objections frequently in your office to stay on your A-game.

CHAPTER 4

Closing the Deal Now

We've learned a lot of awesome techniques to help you get more comfortable, set goals, and learn how to achieve those goals. Because at the end of the day, you're in this to get paid, and that doesn't happen until the deal is closed. So let's get that done.

Remember how we talked about how you have to always be learning? So let's learn how to close. I've listened to so many books on closing like Brian Tracy's "The Art of Closing a Sale". What's cool is, when you're constantly learning, you'll find yourself in the middle of an appointment, and you'll end up applying something you heard or recently learned. It's normally something you've never used before – and it will work.

I'm going to tell you about several situations when I've used closes that are *aggressive*, that most of you will never try. And they've worked on some of my biggest sales ever. But the goal is that you need to be in a constant state of learning. Turn your car into a mobile sales academy. *LEARN*. Knowledge is huge, it can be impactful, and it can teach you what you need to do and when you need to do it. You'll end up retaining that knowledge and will pull nuggets from what you've learned and use it in your experiences and day-to-day happenings. So soak it in.

Below are my top three things that must come before you close a sale.

1. Relationship
2. Value
3. Engagement

Relationship
I like for the relationship to be there. That's why the setup and the warmup are so impactful. You need to have established and created a friendship with your client. You need to know about them. They need to trust you. You need to get along. You will show them that you _actually_ care - they need to know that you do. That's why the relationship and asking those questions about Family, Occupation, Recreation, and getting into your Message (FORM) build on the constant progression of the relationship. This starts as soon as you pull up to the house. And it ends... never. It is a constant progression of relationships and getting to know them.

The relationship piece is the one-piece most agents forget about. It is super impactful and important when you are trying to close deals. The relationship can honestly sway whether they do business with you or not. Just based on the relationship they have with you thus far.

Value
The next piece is the value. The value has _got_ to be there. They've got to see value in what you are talking about. You must build value for the client. I believe in showing benefits; the value in you, the value in the company, and going over all of the benefits of _WHY_ they should do business with YOU.

Go through your presentation, present the benefits, build value in their mind. They need to know that hey, guess what, the value is there. Explain what your benefits are such as a price lock and that it lasts their entire lifetime. They need to know it builds cash value, pays double for an accident, comes with a local representative – all the things that are important to them. They need to know they are choosing the best option. You've got to reassure them. You've got to let them know this is the best option.

Value comes from your confidence in everything you're saying and everything you show them. That makes them eventually feel comfortable with making the decision. So just like the relationship piece, the value has *got* to be there. They have to see the value in everything they're buying. They can like you, but if they like you <u>and</u> the product, they see the value and all the benefits of doing business with you. Then guess what? You'll have a much easier chance of closing them.

Engagement
The final piece here is the engagement piece. This is where I engage with them, the trial closes, the yeses, the assumptive questions, then getting them to say yes. "Hey, I'm assuming you like that." "Is that important to you?" "If you had to choose, which of those benefits do you like the best?" You want to ask the right questions so they are engaging and a part of the process.

If you have a good relationship with them, if they see the value, if you've made them a part of the whole process and they feel engaged, THEN it's time to close. And when you close, you're going to have a higher closing rate because all three of those things are involved and it is easier for them to make a decision IF:

- The *relationship* is there. They like you and trust you.
- They see the *value*. They love the benefits.

- The features are great, everything lines up with what they are wanting.

You have a better chance of getting the close if they have been engaged and they've already said yes 8 thousand times. This goes back to the encyclopedia close that I learned about in one of my audiobooks. I'm not saying you have to ask 8 thousand questions but make sure they are engaged and you're asking the right questions to get them to say yes.

With every 'yes' I'm getting them closer to making a decision. Every engagement piece, every question I ask – I get them to make a *decision,* and I get them closer with each step. That's why I ask questions. And I love the story I shared earlier about the guy in Joplin, Missouri, who didn't know where his policy was. It was the additional question, "If you knew where it was, where would it be?" I was able to get that person to make a decision and that made it easier for me to close him later.

Closing the Sale

Now we've talked about what you need, let's talk about different types of closing strategies. There are *several.* But I want to touch on a couple of key ones that I love to use. The *no call-back close, the leap of faith, trial closes,* and the *3 options close.*

No Call-Back Close

I use this if I can't get them to make a decision and they say they want to think about it. I was with an experienced agent several years ago and we were in a home when the prospect didn't want to pull the trigger.

Mary said, "Hey I need to think about this. This is a big decision."

The premium was a big premium and like $310 a month. It was a lot. I mean it was 300 bucks a month! So the experienced agent looks over at me, and I look at him. I'm closer to Mary than my partner, I'm kneeling right beside her. I'm by her recliner. I had just gotten done going over benefits and the options when she said she wanted to think about it. I like to be in the bubble, in their space, as close as I can without being too close. This is when she said she wanted to think about it.

I said, "You know what? I wish we could let you think about it, but unfortunately, we have an office rule. We don't do call-backs. So, you have everything you need to make an informed decision today. You need it, you want it, you can afford it. Why don't you just take it?"

Mary thought for a second. She said, "Well if I can't call you back then I guess I have to take it." And she did. And we got a $300 a month sale, just like that.

I also had another sale with the *No Call-Back Close*, same situation. They said they needed to think about it. I said all the same stuff and it worked like a charm, but this one was $505 a month. My biggest final expense sale ever. Sometimes I'll even add the verbiage, "You know what, sometimes people want to think about it and they'll pass away a few months later, or a couple of years later. Their family will see our business card on the fridge and realize we didn't help their loved one make a decision. Then their family is mad and blames us. So rather than getting into all the legal ramifications of that, I just want to help you make a decision. So that I don't get in trouble because at the end of the day, it's what you need. And it is best for you to do something. True?" And it works. With the *no call-back close* it's worked on several big sales. I don't like to lose big sales when I'm there. The no call-back close works. If you apply it, you believe in it, and it's aggressive enough, then it will work. And I believe in you.

Leap Of Faith

I love using the *leap of faith* trial close. It has taken someone who was on the opposite of me, nothing I was saying was gelling, to actually MOVING them closer in my direction - it's the best. In these situations, I love using this leap of faith close to get us on the same page.

Here's an example. I was with this couple running an appointment years ago and they said, "You know what, we're not going to give out our bank account. We're just not going to do it. We had a problem with our bank about 40 years ago." Legit 40 years ago, and the couple said, "We haven't given out our bank account information to the city, electrical, sewer, gas, trash, none of it, it doesn't matter. Nobody has it. Nobody has our bank account information and no one takes any money out of our bank account and no one ever will."

Wow. Do you think you could overcome that one?

I said, "Joe and Betty let's play a little game. Let's act like we are in this fairytale world where everything is perfect. I love you and you love me. We've known each other forever. Whatever option you choose is excellent, it is perfect for you. The price you pay, the premium is down to the penny exactly what you would like. And the bank always sends the insurance company the money on the perfect day every month. Again, hypothetical situation, fairytale world, right? Just play along with me. And there is never a mistake. Whatever day you say for the bank to send it, the money gets sent always on that day. It is perfect, excellent and everything is amazing. So if you knew that by doing business with me, that everything was going to be incredible because we are in this fairytale world, you would probably feel more comfortable pulling the trigger on something like that. Wouldn't you?"

And so they said, "Well, yeah. If everything was perfect yeah."

They are over here, I'm over there. So what do I do? It didn't take 8 seconds. It took me about 40-50 minutes of being with them and gaining their trust, using phrases like 'hypothetically,' 'if everything was perfect,' like perfect scenarios, 'hey if you had to take a leap of faith'. From using all of these word tracks I walked out of there with their bank account information. I applied all the things I'm teaching you. Especially *agreeing, assuming* they were going to buy from me, and believing that I was going to get the sale more than they believed they wouldn't buy.

I believed they were going to give me their bank information more than they believed they wouldn't. If you are ever in a very difficult situation, the leap of faith trial close is one I highly suggest trying.

Think about it this way, if their confidence level that they won't give you their bank info is at a 6, and your confidence level has to be an 8. Your confidence has to be more than theirs for you to make that sale. Your believability and your confidence level are *everything* if you're going to make these kinds of sales. And I know you can.

Trial Closes
Some *trial closes* that are super popular and that work for me, are things that get yeses, things like:

"Who's your beneficiary?"
"When the time comes that we need to make sure these things are getting taken care of, who am I going to be delivering a check to?"

Walk them through everything. You want to create a mental picture in their mind of what their plan will look like. The goal is to get them to make a decision. These little *trial closes* are little pieces that get you closer to your goal. They will pay off later when you have to ask questions to get them to make decisions.

Something like, "Hey I'm assuming if everything were to go well and if all this made sense, and you like it, that you'd end up doing business with me today. I'm assuming that's correct, right?"

Those little *trial closes* along the way get them engaged. Here are some more examples: "What's your favorite thing that you've seen so far?" "What do you like the most of what I've shown you?" Those little things, I promise, will pay off. They are *trial closes*. And you've got to have little trial closes along the way. You've got to be asking questions to get yeses and to get their feedback. Trial closing, if you've done enough trial closing along the way, the big close won't seem so big. Target at least 10 *trial closes* throughout.

Another great way to do trial closes is when you are walking them through benefits. You should show at least 5 benefits, and do a trial close before each of the benefits and then after each benefit. You'll explain each one, ask a question and receive a yes, and make sure that this is important to them. You want them to answer with a positive decision. Yes, they like it. And if you're showing them 5 benefits you should easily have 6 trial closes by the time you're done with benefits alone.

3 Options Close

Here I'm going to go through one of my absolute favorite closes. My favorite one is the *3 Options* close. "Alright, Ms. Betty. We talked about those benefits. And the cool thing is, I'm going to show you *3 options* that come with all 5 of those benefits. Especially the price lock which I know you love." Then go through the options in descending order.

- $25,000 for $125/month

- $20,000 for $90/month

- $15,000 for $60/month

'Which of those three do you like the most?' Then I'm going to shut up. No matter how long I have to sit there. I'm not going to say a word until they pick an option. 80% of the stats tell us they are going to choose the one in the middle. But I want to show a range of options and I don't want to show below $10,000. I love using the *3 Options* close because it gets them to make a decision.

Build the relationship with your prospects. Show them the value in you and the product you're selling. When you believe you'd be doing them a disservice if they didn't buy from you, they can feel it. When you have that kind of confidence and believability they can feel it. Keep them engaged throughout by doing *trial closes* all along and then close the deal. Follow these steps and I promise you, you'll see results.

CHAPTER 5

Working the Phone the Right Way

This next chapter is all about the basics of working the phone. I'm talking about being assumptive, using hypotheticals, finishing with questions, using the leap of faith trial closes, pivoting back into control, and leveraging the take-away. There are a lot of great phone basics that you need to know. *EVERYBODY STRUGGLES* with working the phone - but I'm going to show you how to nail it!

Phone vs. In-person
Whether you are working in the field or on the phone you still need lead flow. Lead flow works in the field and it works on the phone too. First, you need to dial them. You can do this in several different ways. You can use a dialer or you can hand dial them. I know several agents who will make $40k-$50k a month by hand dialing all their numbers. But you can't sell anything to anyone if they don't answer the phone. You need to talk to them.

Be persistent by following up. I always recommend 6 calls in 72 hours. I like to utilize my 12-point follow-up system which we will cover later. I also suggest calling with a different phone number alongside double or triple dialing that same person. So if it goes to voicemail and they don't answer, you immediately dial back. This will increase your answer rate. Normally in the field, once you dial them and get an answer you set an appointment.

When doing telesales when they answer the phone, you want to establish control just like with in-person or field sales. The first 30 seconds of being on the phone are critical for establishing control. You need to be in full control right out of the gate. Harvard Business Review says *the first 4-5 seconds are so crucial. In the first 4-5 seconds, you've GOT to be in control.* They have to be listening to me. People's attention spans are shorter than they ever used to be. Harvard Business Review says the first 4-5 seconds will make or break your call so you've got to nail it.

There are primary mistakes that you are making right now that you need to stop making. The number one mistake salespeople make over the phone are literally the first words they say in the introduction. A lot of agents have this really bad habit and I used to have it too. This is how most of us were trained when someone you're calling picks up the phone. We say, "Hello, is this Betty?" or "Hello, are you Betty?" or "Hello, I'm looking for Betty." BUT - No more!!

You can't do that anymore. Instead of "is this", say "Hello Betty". It's more aggressive, it's more confident, it's a better approach and you will end up getting a better response. Think about this, when someone calls you and says, "Is this Cody?" what do I say? "No, you've got the wrong number." or some version of this. Your leads will do this same thing if you don't call them out. You want to start your phone call with control and confidence. THIS. IS. THE. KEY.

Only use your first name. No last name. No company name. You think that's weird right? Dude, it's weird that you do it. I used to make the same mistake. When I started as an intern I was calling for a veteran agent, literally flipping through the phone book cold calling. I didn't realize it back then, but I was making some bad mistakes and not nailing the first 30 seconds.

When you don't nail the first 30 seconds, this gives people the chance to interject and to take control. Then you get the following: "Who is this?" "Why are you calling me?" "I didn't ask you to call me." It gives them the chance to interject and throw out an objection early in the call. In the first 30 seconds, you **can't** allow objections to come up.

You have to establish control of the call immediately.

Instead, start your call like this, "I'm calling about the state-approved expense program. I'm the licensed underwriter that's here to help. Now tell me this..." - then, ask a question and take control.

Taking control early in the call it will make the rest of the call go that much smoother. But if you don't get control and get their attention immediately, within the first 5 seconds, and then the first 60, then you're going to struggle with the rest of the sale. If you are practicing a portion of the call, this is the portion that you need to practice and get your script down. Before you get on your calls, practice your first 60 seconds of your script. After you've gained control, work on qualifying them. You should be able to do that in the first 3 minutes of the call. Focus on building rapport, fact-finding, and then you'll present, close, and cool them off of business.

When you think about your current model from field to telesales, they don't differ that much. Both have lead flow, you dial them, they answer, but in field sales, your next step is setting your in-person appointment. When you show up for that appointment, you build rapport, fact-find, present, close, and cool down. Your average field appointment is 45-60 minutes long. Telesales are the same, but just over the phone. After you've dialed and they answer, you'll start on building rapport, fact-finding to qualify them, you'll then present, close, and cool them down off of business. If you're just transitioning to telesales, it will take some time, it won't be an immediate sale but keep the faith.

Most people jump from field to working the phone under the impression that they might be able to qualify their prospect quicker. Agents end up thinking it will be quicker, simpler, and easier; when in fact getting them to buy over the phone is harder than face to face. Over the phone, it takes them LONGER to know, like, and trust you. Just take your time over the phone and build rapport.

Tips For Working Leads

When it comes to great leads you want multiple avenues to generate those leads. I'm talking digital, direct mail, video strategies, seminars, webinars – I think you get the point. My friend and partner Landon (who is a marketing genius!) and I worked very hard to create our company, Secure Agent Marketing. Our company is an actual insurance marketing agency that has worked in the insurance industry.

Simply put, we understand the language, and know how your prospects search for insurance solutions. Because of this, we generate leads through various social media platforms. Not only that but we create beautiful websites to drive traffic, and content creation to drive brand awareness. Check us out at secureagentmarketing.com to see how we can help you generate more leads.

We are here to help you get leads through every means possible. But once you have the leads, closing the sale is up to you. This is something a lot of agents struggle with but don't worry, I've created a proven system to help you do this.

12-Point Follow-Up System

In this 12-point system we work leads in 3 different ways; by calling them, texting, and emailing them. We call leads 6 times in 3 days. Calling a lead 6 times gives you a 90% chance of contacting them. Remember, you can't sell anything if you don't set an appointment and you can't set an appointment if you don't talk to them. So suck it up and make the phone calls.

A lot of agents struggle with getting in front of people. They don't know how to properly reach out to their contacts and leads. Oftentimes, agents will buy shared leads. Shared leads can be shared with a minimum of 8 other agents. If you don't know when to touch them, how often to touch them, these leads are for nothing. Dude, you paid for the leads! If this is you, I'm going to give you my 3 day, 12-Point Follow-Up System for working leads.

I set up my follow-up to touch my leads 12 times within 72 hours. Now, I'm not saying I don't want to follow up next week, or two weeks from now, or keep trying to door knock after the first 72 hours. Because I do still follow up and work the lead after those first 12 touches. But what I want to do is on day 1, the very first day, I want you to call your lead 3 times by phone, send one text and email, and leave 1 voicemail. So the very first day I want you to call 3 times. I want you to text, email AND I want you to leave a voicemail.

Day number 2: I want you to make 2 calls. You will see a pattern that goes 3, 2, 1. So make 2 calls, send 1 text, 1 email and leave 1 voicemail. Day number 3 – you guessed it. I want 1 call, 1 text, 1 email, and for you to leave 1 voicemail.

So if you add all of those up, 3 calls, a text, and an email that's 5 touches on day 1. Day 2 - 2 calls, 1 text, and 1 email, that's 4 touches. So now you're up to 9 touches in the first 48 hours. Day number 3 - with 1 call, text, and email for 3 touches. Now you're at 12 total touches in the first 72 hours of receiving a lead.

And you say, 'Well dude, why would you do that?' You might even be saying, "I'm used to calling someone one time or maybe emailing them one time." That is probably why your leads are not working for you. Especially if you're buying shared leads. 80% of sales are made between the 5th and the 12th contact. And why do we want to halfway do anything if you know that 12 touches will get results 80% of the time? See my point? DO the 12 touches if you want to see the results. And also, I don't want to wait and I don't want to spread this out over multiple weeks.

The tendency is, that when someone responds that they want information, generally they may not buy from the first or second person who reaches out to them, but they are going to buy it from someone. And even if it is an exclusive lead, the chances are that over half of them are thinking about buying insurance. They might respond to a phone call, a television commercial, a direct mail form, digitally online, or through a referral from a friend. The point is when you have the opportunity to exhaust a lead you paid for, that asked for you to reach out to them ASAP, let's exhaust our leads.

Calling at Different Times of the Day

If you're only calling one time during the day and you're not getting a hold of anyone, guess what? They might not be available then. So try calling at various times during the day and different days of the week. This one is very straight forward but if you do this, it can double your chances of making contact. What happens when we make contact? We can set an appointment or make a sale. No contact, no sale. It's as simple as that.

Triple Dialing/Different Numbers/Scripting

When you call and they don't answer, hang up and call again. When they see the same number calling twice in a row it increases the chance they will pick up the phone. If they don't answer the second time, you can always call one more time, but be sure to leave a voicemail on your third call. If you have not made contact with the number you are using, use a different number. Try implementing this in your regular follow-up routine, as many people won't answer if the number is not from their area code. I know this seems simple enough but not all agents are doing this free and simple tip.

Once they've answered the phone, I utilize my script and begin rapport building and fact-finding by asking open-ended questions. Don't follow your script word for word, make sure to practice, roleplay, and make it your own. Interject *your* personality into it. If it is personal to you, they will feel it. But if you aren't rehearsed and practiced, the second you pause you're dead in the water.

Texting, Email, and Voicemail

We covered this in detail in chapter 3, but I want to remind you again here. Using "a quick question" is especially great when texting. "Good news" works well when sending an email and "drop off" is great for a voicemail. Add these quick tips alongside your script to increase your answer rate.

Other Tips

Assume

One of the basics is being assumptive. Always assume. You must assume everything, assume the sale every step of the way. It is basic and the most elementary of the basics of working the phone tips. You have to assume they are going to answer the phone. You have to assume they are going to love you. You've gotta assume they are going to talk to you for an hour. Assume they are going to buy. Assume they are going to pay right now. You've got to assume they will keep the policy for every day until they pass away.

You have to assume everything because I'm telling you what, if YOU don't assume it, THEY never will. That is the key behind this. Sales are, I believe that you are going to buy more than you believe that you're not going to. That is being assumptive. How assumptive are you? You have to assume everything. You have to assume when you ask a question they are going to answer. Assume they are going to love what you are pitching them, they are on board and ready to roll. They love it, they love you, and they want to do it now. You just have to assume it all.

Here are some examples of this. "I'm assuming that you've loved everything we've talked about, correct?" That's a confident answer, it's *assuming*. What happens is, if you don't believe they like it and that they are going to move forward with it, then they won't. You've got to believe it more than they do. And generally, whose ever belief is higher, wins. They always say "Sell or be sold". You are either selling or getting sold. To take it a step further, I believe in being more sold on my product and on their decision than they are. And when you believe they will make a decision and buy, more than they believe they won't, by *assuming*, then guess what? You end up getting people to make decisions you never would have before.

Some example questions using assume and getting them to make a decision:

"I'm assuming you like this so far, am I right?"

"I'm assuming you'd like to move forward with this right now. Correct?"

"I'm sure we can agree that this is perfect for you. You know what I mean?"

"Have you heard enough to make a decision?"

Then you have the power of 'either-or.' It is less of an ultimatum. If you say, hey do you wanna buy $20,000 they say no. But if you said, hypothetically if you had to choose, would you probably go with 15 or 20 thousand? *Hypothetically*, right? 15 or 20 thousand - the power of either/or, giving them options. People like options. They don't like to be put in a corner, right? When you say, here is your option, this is all you get. No. People like options. They like to feel like they are at least making the decision on their own. If you give them an option you're making the decision for them. If you give them two options, guess what? They are making the decision for themselves. And they are believing and owning what they are about to say, because they said it, not you.

Finish With A Question

The next basic of working the phone tip, you have to finish with a question. One hundred percent of the time on the phone I am finishing with a question. We've talked about control earlier which is a big part of working the phone. You must be in control and the best way to be in control is to ask questions. You must **always** ask a question. It is human nature, when I ask you a question, to do what? To *answer* the question. So why don't we ask *more* questions? I always finish with a question. This is difficult. A lot of salespeople make this really hard, but it's really simple, once you get good at this it's great! But it is hard to always finish with a question on the phone.

It is difficult, it's not natural or normal but once you adopt it and you get good at it, it is amazing how good you can get at maintaining control of the entire call. You will end up closing 30-40% of good conversations by being in control. I always finish with a question 100% of the time.

I do not let my sales team speak over the phone unless they finish with a question because it keeps them in control and it moves the needle. I do not believe in making statements unless I finish with a question. This takes a lot of really honing it in, personalizing it, and making it your own. This is something you need to be role-playing with every single day to get better. If you're going to be on the phone, you need to finish your statements by asking a question. It keeps you in control. It makes your belief higher than theirs. *Always finish with a question.*

The follow-up question makes it seem like it is more important for them to answer but also gives them time to think of a response. So in that instance, I ask a follow-up question. Which most agents never do. Always ask a follow-up question if you don't get the answer you want. Or if they say "I don't know", or "no", "I'm not sure", or "I don't really know". Ask a follow-up question and get the answer that you know is there.

Another thing I do when I'm driving around my neighborhood if I see my neighbors outside I wave at them. If they don't wave back, I will stop my car and continue to wave at them until they wave back. This is because I have trained myself to always get answers to my questions. Using hypotheticals works like crazy by always asking a follow-up question.

So if I'm asking someone, "Which option looks like it would be the best for you?"

"Well, I don't know."

"Well if you had to look at them and choose, what would you say?"

Then they answer. It is *powerful*. It is amazing, it works, and most people are not doing it. Most people don't even know about this.

- Use hypotheticals
- Always ask a follow-up question
- Always get answers to every question you ever ask

Pivoting Back Into Control

Now let's talk about the pivot and pivoting back into control. Imagine you are at the beginning of a path or road, and you need to get to the finish. If you are on this path with them and they give you an objection or they ask a question, think of this as them taking you off the path. And the only way for you to get to the finish line is to pivot and get back on the path. Pivoting back into control.

If they tell you that they are interested in the cost of the product and they aren't sure they can afford it - tell them, "Of course, I'm totally with you." Follow that with a great question, and then promise that you'll get back to their questions in a bit. Here, you'll want to pivot back into control and say, "Tell me this; one of the things we'll need to know to determine how much this is going is to understand your health. How is your health? Ever had any heart attacks? Stroke? Cancer? Talk me through your health? Do you take any medicines?" ← Right here is pivoting back into control. You are getting back on the path to move closer to the finish line. When they try to derail, I want you to pivot back onto the path, to the finish line, and pivot back into control.

I love using hypotheticals. Take them to a hypothetical state. For instance, I love saying the word *hypothetically*. If you ask your wife, "what do you want to do this weekend?" It is a stupid thing to ask because you already know the answer. It's "I don't know." Then you follow it up with, "oh okay well hypothetically, if you had to choose (this is a running joke around the office now because we all use it) what would you say?"

Hypothetically, if you had to choose, what would you say?

Then they stop and think. And they always answer the question. You are used to getting

"I don't know". You're used to getting pushed off. You're used to getting unsure answers or responses of, "well I'm not really sure". I use this in all facets of my life, and by adding "hypothetically if you had to choose, what would you say?"

What do you mean "if they had to choose?" You're making them choose right now. But you're saying hypothetically if you had to choose, you don't have to but if you had to, what would you say? And then they choose. You didn't say they had to choose. But they're going to. Because it works.

The Take-Away

This basic working the phone tip is good. It's powerful, it's incredible, and drives most people nuts. And that is *the take-away close*. When you are in the middle of a sale and you want to take control and get their attention, you use *the take-away* - I love doing this early in the call. "This is a state-approved, final expense program that is meant for people just like you. *However*, I don't know if you'll be able to qualify. It is my job as a local field underwriter to ask the questions necessary to see if you may be able to. A lot of people can't get it but they wish they could. Hopefully, you'll be able to today. So I'm going to ask you some questions and go over everything because again, I don't know if you'll qualify. Are you with me?" That is the take-away close.

And that's a very specific example of the take-away. People move towards things that move away from them. So every once in a while, if you're in a spot where you're stuck, try this close. As a result of you moving the product away from them, it will make them want it more. This is one that you'll want to practice so that when you roll this out of your tool belt, you're prepared and ready to go.

"I don't know *if* you'll be able to get it. But I'm hoping you can. So tell me this"... then ask a question. Use that throughout the call because it's going to drive them nuts. Remember, people, move closer to things that move away from them. The take-away will take it away so they move closer.

You want to be a great salesperson and to do that, you have to be good at both working the phone and face-to-face. But for you to sell anything you have to speak to people. Remember when working leads to make sure you get in your 12 touches from my 12 Point Follow-Up System. This is 12 touches over 3 days via phone call, email, and text. Remember to call at different times of the day, don't be afraid to triple dial and try to call from a different number.

Once you have them on the phone remember to always be *assumptive* - assume they will answer the phone, assume they will love you, and assume they are going to buy from you. Always, always, always *finish with a question!* Remember how I wave at my neighbors? Finishing with a question is a fantastic way to get those trial closes or soft closes in throughout the appointment. Whenever you feel like the prospect has taken over the appointment, *pivot back into control* and try the *take-away* to keep them engaged and moving toward you. If you do these things you'll be killing it in no time.

CHAPTER 6

Your Activity Defines Your Outcome

You are in control of your sales destiny and your outcome as a salesperson. Are you killin' it? Or, are you missing the boat on where you want to be? There's one way to guarantee everything you want, and that's activity. Remember, "if it is to be, it's up to me," and that's a *very* good thing. When you put in the activity necessary to reach your goals, you *WILL* achieve them! But *activity* is the key here. So, let's talk about the things you need to do to make your dreams a reality.

Accountable to Yourself/Accountable to Others
It is one thing for you to believe in your goal. It is another thing to write down your goal. It's an even crazier thing to make them public. I believe in making goals public which is why I've shared my goals with you already.

Another goal I have is to get my companies to make $1M a month. I'm making it public because I'm putting pressure on myself. I know people believe in their goals and believe in themselves. I've found that people attain their goal when they make it public. For example, when we hosted our first 8% Nation Conference, I had no clue what was going to happen. If I wouldn't have made it *public*, I never would have committed to doing it. Holding the conference was a lot of work, a bunch of money, and I wasn't even sure we would be able to pull it off. We didn't know anything about throwing a conference, but as you grow and do new things, you learn. You figure it out as you go. The point of this example is you learn what you need to do to achieve your goals when you make your goals public. We really dug deep to make it a reality, and it worked because we've held a conference every year since 2018. But you have to start by making it public. I can't say it enough, **_you must make your goals public!_**

The best way to keep yourself accountable is by having accountability partners or mentors. These people need to be where you want to be. They're more successful, they have it figured out, they know what they're doing, and thus, can hold you accountable. The idea is to share your goals, whatever they are, with your partners or mentors so that people know your goal and they're going to hold you accountable.

For instance, if someone I know has a weight loss goal and they're not doing things to get them closer to their goal, then I'm going to tell them. If I'm an accountability partner or a mentor - if I care and they want me to share, then I'm going to tell them. Because they're not getting closer to their goal. They're screwing up. They're making a mistake. They aren't serious. When you make it public, people focus on your goal and they watch you. They watch to see if you are going to be disciplined enough and consistent enough to hit it. So have some accountability partners - your wife, your friends, your mentor, your coworkers. Have a mentor to track everything with you and keep you accountable and honest to follow through on this goal. One thing I did at an early age, is if I had a contest or I wanted to make $100k I would write down, _hey I'm going to make 100 grand this year._ I wrote it down. I signed it. My father signed it and I hung it up in my office. That's accountability.

Having a Goal And Breaking Down The Numbers

GOOOOOOAAAAALLLSSSS

Goals are the most powerful thing you can have. I love thinking big and setting crazy targets. What do I *want* to achieve and how do I get there? Breaking down the numbers of your targets, so you know what you need to do every step of the way to hit those targets. And then I take *action*. I make it *public*. I have accountability partners. I make myself accountable, I hold myself accountable. I put a lot of pressure on myself. *Goals* are the one thing that can take you to another level. Without goals, I would not be where I am today. So I'm super excited to introduce this chapter, let's dive in.

There isn't a bad way or a wrong way but I love setting short-term goals. Like a goal for this week, especially if I'm a salesperson. Or, maybe a goal for this year. Or even a long-term goal. Some of the goals I have, that I write down every single day are about all six of my companies. I also have some personal goals that I've set; owning a jet, and traveling the world to help every salesperson. I believe in writing lofty goals. So that is one of the things I do. I think short-term, this year, and long-term.

Goals are super important but you have to know how to set them. So figure out what YOUR goals are. Take a second right now and think about your personal goals, goals you want to hit every week to hit your annual goal. Like when I was a brand new agent my goals were:

1. To make $100k my first year as an agent.

2. To earn $1 Million before I was 30 years old.

By the time I was 28 those two goals were achieved simply because I set them, broke down how to get to them (set up a system to achieve them), and had accountability.

Remember to think big. When I talk about thinking big, I mean *THINKING BIG.* Most people think waaay too small. What do you want to happen? And I don't care how big it is. If you write it down, if you personalize it, if you believe it, and you remind yourself of it *every single day* - no matter how BIG it is, you've got a way better chance of achieving it. So my challenge to you throughout this whole chapter is to *THINK BIGGER.*

Think bigger than you've ever thought before. Dinky, little bitty goals won't get you anywhere. If you write down 50k, I'm going to come through this book and shake you, because this chapter is ALL about thinking big, taking yourself to a whole 'nother level, and doing more. You have way more potential than you realize. I didn't realize I would be where I am at 30, and when I look back in 10 more years I'll probably laugh at where I was. I'm telling you what, *THINK BIG, BIGGER THAN YOU'VE EVER THOUGHT* and I promise you it will pay off. So do not overlook goals. Now that you know how to set them and that you should be setting them, we are going to go into more detail.

Target

You *must* set a target to achieve whatever it is you want to achieve. I believe in setting big targets often and hitting those targets. What's your target? It's hard to have a goal if you don't have a clear target. Have a clear-cut target like I did when I first started in the business - making $100 grand my first year. I did it in 8 months. Or, when I wanted to scale one of my brands to 1 million dollars a month. That is a target.

You have to have a target. It has to be clear. It has to be concise. You have to be able to understand it. And it doesn't even matter if it is achievable. As long as you believe it is achievable, who cares what other people think? Set that target and go get it. But it has to be a clear target you can go get.

Just because you've said you have a target and you've said it out loud doesn't mean you are going to achieve it. You won't unless you break down the numbers, and you know what to do to get you to that target. If you don't do that then it doesn't matter. There are a lot of people on planet Earth that say, "Hey I'm going to do this (you probably know somebody, I'm thinking of somebody right now) I promise I'm going to do this". But they never break it down and they never put any action into it. So yes, you can set a target. But you have to break down those numbers after you set a target. What does it look like?

Break It Down
Let's say it's a quarter of a million dollars. I'm going to use that because I think that is the new 100k. If you've never made 100k then make it 100k. But I feel like 100k ten to twenty years ago is more like 200 - 250k now. So when I think about making $250,000 I think about how to break it down. Like we talked about before, divide your target by 50 weeks so you get two weeks off in the year. That's $5,000 a week. If you work 5 days a week that's $1,000 a day. Right now you're probably thinking "Oh, I can make $1,000 a day". But 8 seconds ago you were thinking, "I can't make a quarter of a million dollars this year." If you can make a thousand dollars in a day, then you *can* make a quarter of a million dollars in a year. It goes back to consistency. But you *have* to break down those numbers. But I mean, break them down even further. KNOW. YOUR. NUMBERS.

How do you make $1,000 a day?

Set/Sit/Sell
Let's say your average sale is $1,000. Guess what? You need 1 sale a day per day. In general, the average closing rate for salespersons is 50%. So guess what? You need to see two people per day if these are *your* numbers. Maybe, you need

to set 3 appointments. Maybe two of the three appointments you set will show up, and then maybe you'll sell one worth a grand if that is your actual average. And if it isn't then you need to see more and sit with more. But in this case: 3, 2, 1. It is all about the numbers.

Then how do you set 3 every day? How do you set 15 every week (or whatever your numbers look like)? I want you to break them all the way down so you know your numbers. Let's keep going with this example. Let's say you call 100 people and speak to 30 of them. From that 30, you can set your 15 appointments. So again, when you know what your numbers are, you will more easily get to your goal.

You also need to figure out how much you make per dial and per door knock. Break those numbers down. It isn't rocket science. 5 grand divided by 100 dials... everyone I know can do that. Come on man! That's 50 bucks per dial. So what you're telling me, Cody, is if I pick up the phone, I just made $50? In this example, that's correct. In this example that's exactly what I'm saying. So break down the numbers. Know it down to the dial. Down to the door knock. Down to what you need to do every single day and every week to hit that target. And it makes it so much easier if you know it and if you are *consistent* with it. This is my *Triple S System*. Set. Sit. Sell. Set 15 appointments, sit with 10, and sell 5.

Take Action

You've set the goals, you've crunched the numbers, you know what you need to do, right? Here is the problem with all of this. Now it is up to you to create the action. Anyone can have a goal, a dream, a target, and figure out their numbers. But if they aren't *taking the action necessary*, nothing will happen toward that goal. And do you know why? Because their work ethic sucks. They're lazy. They aren't serious about it and they won't do whatever it takes. All of the things we talked about earlier are coming back full circle. If you want your goals to happen, you have to make them happen. I don't want you to just do all this work and not take action and succeed.

When you figure out what you want your income to be, then ACTUALLY DO IT. I'll use myself as an example because it is easy to do. I hate running, but I finished a 5k, then a half marathon. I trained for and completed a triathlon. I haven't worked this hard consistently since college, since basketball. I didn't think I could. Or maybe I thought I could, and maybe I was just being lazy. Maybe my work ethic wasn't high and tight and right. At the end of the day, it takes discipline to achieve success. Figure out what you need to do and then just make the decision to do it. Don't let anything get in the way. *Take action. Be consistent. And just freakin' do it.*

Track It Every Day
You have to track your goal. We've talked about accountability, writing down your goal, signing it along with your accountability partner, and speaking it in public – that is all accountability. Another thing I do is to track progress using a whiteboard I have hanging up in my office. It's where I can see it every day and I can track progress. So if you want to make $100k in 2021 then it would start at zero and you track this on your whiteboard. Then every 5 or 10 grand, move the meter. Not only are you tracking it, but you can visually see your progress. It is better when it's trackable, it is visual, and you can see it every single day. Since you are writing it down and you are also seeing your progress. Then you can look and say, "Hey do I need to do more?" Or, "Hey I'm ahead," just don't slow down when this happens, finish it sooner instead. It is a better story when you can do it in 8 months instead of 12 months, trust me. I know the feeling.

I've been to two world series because I won an insurance sales contest with an insurance company I used to work for. Every year I was with that company I made that trip because

I set a goal to make it happen. I had accountability, I spoke it into existence, I tracked my activity, and I put in the effort. This wasn't because I was the most experienced or the best salesperson. It was because I tracked it. And I said, *"Hey, I'm going to make it."* And I made it public. Everybody thought I was nuts. But I didn't care because I knew I was going to achieve it. I was the only person in my entire office to ever be able to do that because I believed it. TRACK IT.

When I was trying to make the world series my wife would build a baseball field and I would move a picture of me dressed up as a baseball player around the bases. It is visual, it's trackable. Yeah, it's cheesy. But at the end of the day, if it works, and it gets you closer, who cares?! So track your goal meticulously so that you can visually see your progress along the way.

Set your goals. Think **_BIGGER_**. Hold yourself accountable. Speak it into existence by putting it out there in public. Get a mentor or accountability partner. Break down your numbers to achieve your goal and TRACK IT. Big things are coming, I promise you.

CHAPTER 7

What's Next: Building a Sales Team

If you follow everything in this book, you'll be killing it in six figures, and the trick to get to seven figures? Build a team. I'm extremely excited to go over everything we do. You need to be thinking about how you scale your ideas and thoughts.

From recruiting, hiring, paying, training, holding people accountable, watching activity, and how you can continue to get better at what you're already doing. Everything that we know: How I keep the energy up, how to motivate your team, everything that we do, I'm going to share it with you. Not only will you learn unbelievable content but it will get you thinking bigger.

Building a sales team is valuable. It's important. Our sales team is the most profitable part of our business, and it can be for you too. But there are a lot of ins and outs of this whole sales team thing that you may or may not know, that you need to know. And I'm going to make sure you know. I want to show you how to build a massive freaking sales team.

Building Your Team
When you're trying to build a sales team the number one thing is you have to *be* a leader and *lead by example*. So if I'm not willing to work out every day, wake up early every day,

train every day, and all this kinda stuff, then I can't expect my team to. Cause that's just dumb. Also, I feel like we are trying to make them better every day. I have them give me their objections, we write 'em down. I give them sentences to say, we work on closing, fact-finding, and we roleplay as a team, either back and forth or through one of our competitive games. Every. Single. Day.

The biggest problem with sales teams is, most sales teams are moving backward over time. The owner doesn't realize it but the sales team is moving backward over time. The truth is in the numbers. The numbers don't lie, and when I saw that our sales team's numbers were not growing, sometimes going backward, or about even, I knew it was my fault.

What happens along the way and what is really easy for a sales manager, leader, or owner to do, is to say, "These guys just aren't me. They aren't as good as me. They don't work as hard as me." It's really easy to blame other people. Like once when I was traveling and I was blaming the audience for a lack of energy when really I just wasn't bringing it. It is the same thing. That taught me the result is 100% within my control. In all areas of life. And my dad even said it to us at one point, "Inspect what you expect." That is when I started inspecting what I expected to happen.

During this inspection is when I started noticing lower sales numbers, I thought, *oh my gosh what's the problem here?* I was about to go on vacation for a week so I decided I would let them try something new while I was gone. Really it was more of a test for them. I wanted to see if they were lazy or if they really want it. I thought I'll give them one week to do whatever the heck they want, and show up whenever they want. BUT, I'm going to make it the most competitive week of all time. I'm talkin' tons of incentives, thousands in cash, and I even allowed them to sell leads for the lowest amount I had ever sold them for, from a sales team perspective.

Anything they wanted, I gave it to them. Anything they wanted, I just did it, which isn't like me. But I wanted to see who really wants this thing. By doing that we had the biggest week we've ever had, by far. This taught me that it wasn't the sales staff.

What I realized was that other things are going on here.... Now, do I need to leave the lead prices super low forever? No. Do I need to get crazy with incentives every week? No. Do they need incentives? Yes. But I thought *okay, there's more that I can do to help make my team successful.* So we made some changes when I got back from vacation.

I moved them all right outside of my office. Not so I could micro-manage them because I don't have time for that. But so I can hear them and I can see them. I added some tiered bonuses to incentivize them. And I decided I'm going to train them every day from 8:30 am - 9:00 am and from 1:30 pm - 2:00 pm. The plan was, during this time, we are going to do three things. We are going to train 'em, pump up our energy - because it sucks, and we are going to role-play. I even made sure they had access to play music during the day because it kept the hype going.

But sometimes when we try to implement a structured environment leaders will do things like becoming a drill sergeant, get onto people all the time, and take away things like the music. But then the culture sucks and nobody is happy. This is something I've had to learn the hard way. Some people you can jump on and take things away and that will work. Other people will shut down. So you have to learn what motivates them and understand the best way to communicate with each of your team members. When you can properly communicate with them, you can properly create a relationship and an environment that will flourish.

I've also tried to take myself out of the *I'm their boss* role and more into *I'm here to help them make more money* and increase sales. So I need them to be happier, more motivated, and I need them to improve. All of this has been a hard, hard shift for me.

Communication

I worked on this a lot. While I'm not going to let them get away with stuff, I am going to have a little looser leash, slightly. But above all else, I'm going to be positive. And if I notice a trend I'm going to let them know, "Hey dude, I'm going to need you focused because when you're focused you're really good. And when you're showing up late it looks bad. You're a leader, you're doing well. When you have 80 dials you crush it. I'm telling you if you haven't seen yourself improve I have, and I can help you make 6 figures this year. I just need you to wake up. I can't want it more than you. I'm here to help. If you have questions, come to me. If you need me to KO a call I'm here."

They also come to me with ideas now. Before, I was the corporate boss that wouldn't let them sell something at a discount. Or I wouldn't let them bring an idea to me because I *know what's best and I don't need your opinion.* Now, I'm open to ideas. They've given me several ideas that help us create a lot of custom filters and custom additions and now, agents can add to their order. But I didn't allow that stuff before. Now, when people ask me, "hey can I do this?" I allow them to do it.

What We Do With Our Sales Teams

Energy

One of the big things people struggle with the most is getting their team motivated when they are unmotivated and picking up the energy and the culture when it sucks. And we've had it happen here.

You have to enthuse your people. You've gotta get them excited, motivate them and get their energy up. We like to start off with push-ups. Someone throws out a number like 25 or 30 - none of this 10 business, nobody has time for that. We've gotta get that energy *UP*. I ask who's leading? Someone steps up, we all drop down, even me, and then we count them out together. When we're done we bring it in for the chant. Hands in on the count of three.... "Sales!" You've gotta get them out of breath. We do that twice a day and if you don't do those things, you need to start doing this. Sales training, role-playing, energy, team chants... get everyone excited.

I've found ways to increase their confidence and their energy with games like the circle closing challenge and the pick your objection game. For the circle closing challenge, we get the team in a circle. I'll say a question, and the person standing next to me won't respond to the question but will simply ask another question. And this happens all the way around the circle and keeps going. If someone hesitates, or they screw up the question, or they say something they've already personally said, or if they repeat what the person previously just said then they get kicked out of the circle.

You keep going from 8, 6, 5 people whatever it is until you get to, head to head, down to 2 people. You're going back and forth just asking each other questions until 1 person wins. Doing this really gets their brain moving faster and it gets them talking faster. What I've learned about salespeople is when you're in control, you make the sale. To be in control you've gotta think on your feet. You've gotta be ready when someone asks you a question. And you have to be willing to ask a question every time along the way. So by doing this game, they're more confident, they're better, they're awake, their energy is up, it's competitive and it fuels them first thing in the morning. So by the time 9:00 am rolls around, they are on a high and ready to go, when before they were half asleep. The added bonus is we're all making sales early in the morning and gunning from the start.

Training

Since we are training twice a day now, every single day, I even restructured lunches. They used to all go at different times. But I want to train them again at 1:30 for another 30 minutes. If they are doing different lunches someone may be on a call during training so I'm like hey, you leave at 12:30 you come back by 1:30 and we are training from 1:30-2.00. Having this set time has provided more organization and structure too.

If it is good enough to do once, it is good enough to do every day. This is why we train every day twice a day. And we set the expectation. When you're in this meeting you're going to be paying attention, taking notes, you aren't going to be late or on your phone.

If they are on the phone with a customer, and the meeting is about to start I will walk over, take the phone, and say, "I'm so sorry but I'm going to have to call you back," then hang up. This time is the most important part of the day. It is important to set the tone and to set it early with your sales team.

We also track their activity daily. We have leaderboards around the office tracking their activity so we know every second of every day what's going on. I wanna know dials, conversations, talk time, sales, and revenue. So we are literally tracking their activity constantly. We also have a whiteboard in our office and we keep track of their week on a whiteboard. Everybody has to go up and put in their dials, conversations, sales, and money at the end of each day. They have to physically walk up before they leave and fill it out.

Since we are tracking all this activity we can see daily numbers, weekly numbers, monthly numbers, the previous week and month and we can track that for every single sales representative in our office.

After tracking activity, we've already talked about this but we train every day. When we train, we use my CA Sales

System - it has over 450 modules and quizzes and we use this twice a day. My Sales System is specifically built for sales teams to plug in and train every single day and it's me on all the videos. We also have a monthly live Q&A that is group style.

We also role-play. By now you know how much I love it and how valuable it is. We always role-play on something specific, something small like an objection, a certain phrase, it's how to ask for the business with "x", it's when the client says this "XYZ", what do you say? We train on our intro pitch so when we get on the phone the first thing we're not rusty. Have you ever made a call and after it was over said, "dude I screwed that up". I felt rusty, that sucked, and I hope I never do that again. When this happens, guess what, you just lost money. And last time I checked we are still operating a business, not a charity because we want to make money. So we train every single day. We are improving every single day because that's the point, right?

After training, we jump into some energy activity: jumping jacks, push-ups, squats, a run around the building - something. Again, I need their energy up. If they woke up at 7:30 and they got to the office at 8:30, which I consider sleeping in by the way, then what do they usually do when they get to the office? Maybe they haven't had coffee yet, they're running late, or they're stressed out. Whatever it is, I need to wake them up. They can't float through the day and finally wake up at 10 or 11 o'clock. It just doesn't work, that's dumb. After the energy activity we do a little "1, 2, 3 Sales!" or like a Rick Flair "wooo" on Wednesdays, I don't know. They change it up. The point is, it's something to get them up, to get them going and jacked up.

This changes your culture. It changes the energy in the room. It's fun. Because no one wants to go to an office, sit in a cubicle, and be all alone with no music, and no supervision - whether they say they want supervision or not, they do I promise you because when they have supervision they make more money.

And this instills confidence. Anyone on my team could field any call from any person - I will challenge them. They are prepared. They are ready. I don't care what you throw at them. You could say, "Hey I hate your guts." They will respond with, "Perfect. I'm with you. You know what? Most people do until they try our product and then they love us. How many leads would you like to start with?" I'm telling you they are prepared and ready.

You can still do it remotely

Just like with sales you have to be ready for whatever life is going to throw at you. With all the amazing technology we have like Zoom, we can work completely remotely. So if this is you, one of the first things you need when you are selling insurance from home is good equipment. If you have a slow computer, a crappy headset, you know whatever it is, you need good equipment. I always like a quick running computer, at the minimum two monitors, and a noise-canceling headset.

After good equipment, you also need to eliminate distractions around you. It's going to be really easy to get distracted when you're selling from home. You might have kids running around, your wife, your dog, you get the point. So just lock yourself in a room for a couple of hours. Get focused on getting great at working the phone. Some people are already good at it but a lot of people aren't.

Outlined below are the things you need to be good at working the phone:

1. Lead flow

   - Fill the pipeline
   - Incoming interest

2. High Activity
   - Dials
   - Effort
3. Follow up
   - 12 touches in first 72 hours
     - 6 of those touches are phone calls
4. Script/system
5. Control
6. Relationship Building
   - They know you
   - They like you
   - They trust you
7. Assume

Anyone can work the phone. Anyone can do this from home, or from anywhere really. You just have to follow the steps because they work. But for a minute let's get back to the numbers because if you don't know your numbers and your activity then it doesn't matter where you're working from.

Tracking Your Team

I noticed that my team wasn't making sales for the first hour and a half to two hours typically. I noticed this trend because I track numbers for everything for every person. It is just something I've always done because I know it helps. When I saw that I started asking them, "Hey what time did you wake up this morning?" If they just woke up 30 minutes before work they didn't have their body and mind going yet. As Bryan Tracy always said, you have to wake up at least 2 hours before any sales-related activity, or any business meeting at all.

We also run a Profit and Loss financial statement on each salesperson every month. When I have a solid sales team, they are financially making me money. If you don't make me money we're not going to keep them. If they haven't gotten to where I need them to be in the first 90 days we're going to part ways. But part of helping them to reach their goals and to make me money is being able to break it all down and track it.

What do I need them to do to be successful? I can't expect them to read my mind so I tell them and show them the expectations through tracking results. And we track everything.

We track their dials, talk time, number of appointments set, appointments ran, sales, and revenue. We set goals for each month. We look at all the numbers and I keep a tally of what they are doing for the month and if they're on pace for their goal. I also keep last month's numbers up so everybody can see them. On our sales board, we change the order on the board every week. So if you sucked one week you move to the bottom of the board. If you were the champ last week you're on top. This helps to keep that competitive nature up and if you're not competitive you don't need to be in sales anyways.

If you want your team to be successful remember you have to be a leader and lead by example. Make sure you get your workout in, get up early, and train every day.... I don't just mean train your team every day either. I mean you need to be part of those activities. Play the games with them, do push-ups with them, get yourself and them psyched at the same time. No one wants to work for someone who isn't willing to do the things they are asking you to do themselves.

Remember the numbers don't lie, people do, but the numbers don't. If you aren't tracking your team's numbers you have to start doing it. It is a must! Track everything and make it visual then you have to hold them accountable for their performance. You aren't making excuses for them so don't make excuses for yourself either. You are the reason they aren't performing. So make your expectations clear. Be positive and communicate to them when they aren't hitting the mark and let them know they need to improve. See what help they might need from you and make yourself available to support them. I want to encourage you to have a fun office environment and to continue to push. When you do this you'll see the results.

CHAPTER 8

Bonus! How to Get to Your First $10k a Month

You're a new agent and you wanna make $10k your first month. I made just over 9 grand my very first month as a salesperson. It wasn't 10, but I'm going to tell you exactly what I did to make 9. Are you sitting there thinking, "Dude I wanna make $9k!" Now, I want you to imagine if you got to $10k a month consistently. Not only would you be making six figures (and maybe a lot more), but you'd have *proven* to yourself and others that you can do it. Let's get you there.

Month one, as a brand-new agent, where do you start? What should you do? First of all, there should be a goal ($10k), but I want you to think and focus on one thing. Your whole focus needs to be on setting appointments. If you are going to make $2,500 per week to get to your $10k a month, then you have to get in front and talk to people. Right? But how many appointments do you need to set? In order to know that, we need to break down the numbers.

Let's say your average sale is $500 per sale. If you need to make $2,500 per week at $500 per sale, the math says you need 5 sales per week. So here is what I would do looking at the "set, sit, sell" model we covered earlier.

- Set - 15 + appointments (⅓ of the appointments will fall off before you sit with them)
- Sit - 10+ (as a new agent, if your closing rate isn't at 50% or you don't have prior sales experience then you may need to sit with more than 10)
- Sell - 5 (closing about half the appointments that you sit with)

Or your model above could look like this:

- Set - 20
- Sit - 12 to 13
- Sell - 5

In order to get your 5 sales, your numbers could be less or they could be more for your set and sit. You have to figure out what those numbers are for *you*. I recommend you use the first week and the second week as a gauge for what those numbers should be in the future. Remember this is all based on your average sale being $500. So again, your numbers could be less or more so you need to take that into account too. This is just an example of how to think through the numbers.

Making sure you hit your 'sets' is the number one priority every single week. Every single week you need to think about that. Think about if you've set enough appointments for the week. Focus on "hitting your sets" because if you hit your 'sets' you will hit your 'sits' and most likely your 'sells'. $10k this month HERE WE COME!

Now I want you to start thinking specifically, how do you set the 15-20 appointments per week? How do you make that happen? The first thing I would do as a brand new agent is making a 'hit list'. On this list, I would write down

100 people who know me, or I know them. On the list, you need a name and number. Then you need to attack that list. Explain to them you're now a part of the insurance industry and you're going to come over and see if you can save them money. Attacking that hit list is one of the big ways I got out of the gate quickly and made a lot of money fast. We use this all the time. Any time we come up with a new idea in the office we attack a hit list with that new idea. So think about this hit list, it should be *at least* 100 names. But I want to challenge you right now to get to 500.

Doing these things your very first month is an *absolute must* if you want to make that 10 grand. It is a lot harder than you'd think and pretty rare, but I promise you it can be done, so get started on making that list. Once you have your list it's time to make those calls.

When you are making calls don't just call the 100+ (or 500 if you took me up on my challenge) people on the hit list and call it good. You need to be making calls to other people too. These calls will be to leads, aged leads, even some cold calling as well. Add in this activity so you're adding on to everything you're already doing. Because what happens when you're making calls one week, you're just focusing on the hit list, and it doesn't go so well? Then you have nothing else to do. The point of this is to keep your activity up by calling those new leads, aged leads, and cold calling.

Speaking of activity, you need to find some additional activity to fill your time. The number one reason agents fail is because they don't get in front of enough prospects. They don't get in front of enough prospects because they don't have enough activity on a *consistent* basis. Consistency is key. So what do you need to do to absolutely make this happen? What are those steps?

These are the 5 steps that you need to take:

1. Set a Target - In this case, we know our target is $10k

2. Break Down the Numbers - now you know what numbers you need to hit for your target to be a reality. If you don't break down the numbers it is like going on a trip without a destination, it's weird and you won't get anywhere.

3. Hit Your Sets - if you don't hit the amount of 'sets' you need, you won't hit the 'sits' or 'sells'.

4. Do ***NOT*** Lower Your Activity Level - once you hit your sets it is natural for people to want to lower their activity level. Don't do it. Or if you aren't hitting your sets people start to slack. If you aren't hitting your sets, you have to RAISE your activity level. Make more calls to get more sets.

5. Raise the Goal - do **NOT** lower your goal just because you have lower sales or lower activity. You should actually raise it because clearly the goal is too easy and you aren't putting in the effort to get there. So challenge yourself even further by raising your goal.

Doing these steps is what it takes to make $10k a month. Are you willing to do the steps? Are you willing to put in the work? I'll even give you an additional bonus step right here. When you are working on your hit list don't forget that they already know you, they like you, they love you, and they care about you (because you already know them). They also know people that need help with this. ***REFERRALS.*** This is the biggest lost art in the insurance industry because most people never ask. My dad, Brian Askins is incredible at getting referrals, and the first step is to ask.

I'm telling you to ask! If you will just ask, you will receive. Think about it. The biggest reason people don't make sales, get referrals, cross-sell, and anything else that they want, is because they don't ask. Ask and you shall receive.

You always have to set your goal or set a target. Then hone in on that target by figuring out how many appointments you'll need from my "set, sit, sell" model. You always have to break down your numbers to be successful. So be sure and make that hit list and make sure you exhaust it. Do not forget to ask those people who love you for those referrals, because they are dying to help you out. Constantly be tracking your activity and making sure you are doing whatever it takes to set those appointments. If anything, increase your activity level to reach your target. And whatever you do under no circumstance should you slack off on your activity level or lower your goal. Do all these steps and you're on your way to make $10k your first month.

QR Code

ACKNOWLEDGMENTS

To Lauren:

My wife, Lauren, is my biggest cheerleader; she encourages me to take risks, think big, and dream even bigger. She believes more in me than I even believe in myself. My success which is now OUR success, would not be where it is if she wasn't in my life, that I can assure you. She has the biggest heart of anyone I know; she cares and thinks about our employees first before anything else. I can tell you that the moment she got on board with our dreams and embraced my craziness is the moment when we started to skyrocket. Everyone needs a Lauren in their life. Love you, babe!

To My Parents:

My personal confidence comes from my parents, Brian and Patti Askins. I don't know how they became such perfect parents, but they were and still are absolutely unreal. As a kid, they made me believe that I could do anything in life. So when I grew up, I continued to believe that I could accomplish anything in life. They spoke positivity, encouraged me, and I was grateful to have an incredible childhood. They encouraged creativity, didn't stifle it. Because of this, it absolutely transferred into my career and professional life. Because of my parents, I believe that you can accomplish anything as long as you believe in yourself.

To Landon:

Landon is a marketing freak who has innovated, elevated, and impacted our client experience with Secure Agent Marketing into something extremely special. When I first met Landon, you could just tell there's something different about this dude. It started when he was managing my Google Ad Words and transitioned into us becoming good frings along with our wives. We would go eat sushi together and over time, we decided to create a unique opportunity to create a marketing company together. And then Secure Agent Marketing was born, and we've never looked back. If you ever get a chance to work and speak with Landon, you won't regret it. Appreciate you, buddy.

To Steve:

To Steve, you are one of the most hard working and committed guys I have ever met. Since the time you started working with me you've been so extremely loyal to the successes of the team. Steve will do anything and everything for anyone. Lauren and I are both so extremely grateful for all of the big and small things this man has done for us. Steve, I appreciate you and look forward to our continued friendship.

To Andy:

I get a lot of credit, but our whole team runs smoothly when I'm flying around the country training teams, and I've gotta give a lot of thanks to Andy, our COO. Andy handles the operations, and he plays a huge role in hiring the right people. I used to think I would just hire someone, and good things would happen. But I realized that that actually hurts. With Lauren's love of having a dynamic company culture and Andy focusing on building the right team, he's made an enormous impact on what we're doing at HQ. I appreciate you, buddy, and I see you. Keep up the great work.

To the Cody Askins and Secure Agent Marketing Team Members:

We couldn't do it without you. Everything we're doing right now is exciting and motivating, but what we're doing right now is NOTHING compared to what we'll be doing in the future. You can't do anything without a team, and when I started this, it was just me, Lauren, and a cameraman. Our team just keeps growing and I want it to go up from here.

We have a team that plans everything we do and makes all of it happen. Let's give them a hand — the better the team, the better the results. The better the environment you create, the better your team will become. We are so thankful and proud of our team. I value each one of you, and I'm so proud and grateful for what you're doing. Let's go, guys!